Native Grasslands

CIRCLE OF LIFE

Native
Grasslands

Alexandra Siy

DILLON PRESS
New York

Maxwell Macmillan Canada
Toronto

Maxwell Macmillan International
New York   Oxford   Singapore   Sydney

In memory of my mother

Acknowledgments

I would like to thank Catherine Gray of the California Nature Conservancy and Ken Greenwood of the Oklahoma Nature Conservancy for providing me with information and photographs of the Carrizo Plain and the Tallgrass Prairie Preserve.

Thanks also to Wes Jackson and Jon K. Piper of the Land Institute for suggestions and information.

For additional photographs thanks go to Lavonda Walton of the U.S. Fish and Wildlife Service, Tim McCabe of the U.S.D.A. Soil Conservation Service, Betty Branch and Anita Daniels of the U.S.D.A., and Susan Myers of the National Park Service.

Photographic Acknowledgments

The photographs are reproduced through the courtesy of Tim Johnson; Library of Congress; Nature Conservancy of Oklahoma; Harvey Payne; Smithsonian Institute, National Anthropological Archives; Soil Conservation Service / Tim McCabe; Lynn M. Stone; U.S. Department of Agriculture; and U. S. Fish and Wildlife Service/Luther Goldman, David B. Marshall, William Radke.

Library of Congress Cataloging-in-Publication Data

Siy, Alexandra.
    Native grasslands / by Alexandra Siy.
        p.   cm. — (A Circle of life book)
    Includes index.
    Summary: Examines the plant and animal life of the prairie grasslands of North America and how they are interdependent.
    ISBN 0-87518-469-3
    1. Prairie ecology—United States—Juvenile literature. 2. Prairie ecology—Juvenile literature.
    3. Indians of North America—West (U.S.)—Juvenile literature. 4. Prairies—United States—History—Juvenile literature. [1. Prairie ecology. 2. Ecology.] I. Title II. Series.
    QH104.S58 1991
    574.5' 2643—dc20   91-18412

Dillon Press
Macmillan Publishing Company
866 Third Avenue
New York, NY 10022

Maxwell Macmillan Canada, Inc.
1200 Eglinton Avenue East
Suite 200
Don Mills, Ontario M3C 3N1

Macmillan Publishing Company is part of the Maxwell Communication Group of Companies.
First edition

Printed in the United States of America
10   9   8   7   6   5   4   3   2   1

Contents

▼

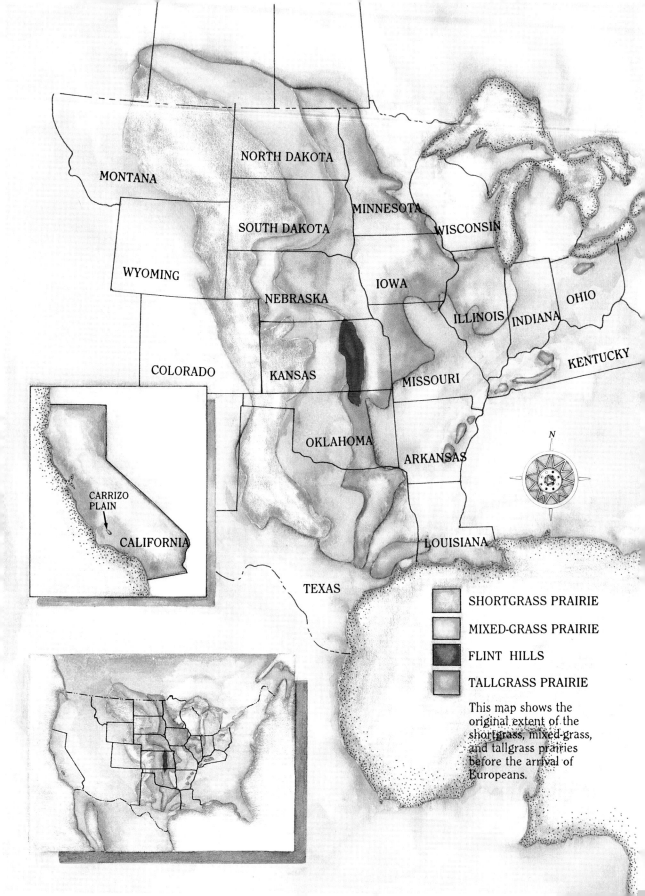

MONTANA

NORTH DAKOTA

SOUTH DAKOTA

MINNESOTA

WISCONSIN

WYOMING

IOWA

NEBRASKA

ILLINOIS

INDIANA

OHIO

COLORADO

KANSAS

MISSOURI

KENTUCKY

CARRIZO
PLAIN

CALIFORNIA

OKLAHOMA

ARKANSAS

LOUISIANA

TEXAS

N

SHORTGRASS PRAIRIE

MIXED-GRASS PRAIRIE

FLINT HILLS

TALLGRASS PRAIRIE

This map shows the
original extent of the
shortgrass, mixed-grass,
and tallgrass prairies
before the arrival of
Europeans.

Native Grasslands

▼

Facts

Location: Native American grasslands, also known as prairies, exist as small "islands" in the midwestern and western parts of the United States.

Climate: Grasslands are dry, averaging 4 to 24 inches of rain a year.

Ecology: Perennial grasses are the most common kinds of plants. The few trees that grow on the grasslands are limited to riverbanks and prairie edges. Fire and grazing animals play an important part in grassland ecosystems.

History: At one time in the earth's history, grasslands covered one-half of the earth's surface. Before the arrival of Europeans, grasslands covered all of the Great Plains (from Canada to Mexico and east of the Rocky Mountains to the Mississippi River); grasslands also covered the valleys in California.

Human History: Native Americans lived on the grasslands for ten thousand years. As the grasslands were turned into farms by settlers in the eighteenth and nineteenth centuries, Native Americans were forced off the prairies and onto reservations.

Human Way of Life: Almost all of the native grasslands in the United States have been plowed over and changed into agricultural lands.

Global Importance: Grasslands are biologically diverse eco-systems. The plants native to grasslands have provided the world with its basic food grains. In the future, grassland plants may provide new food crops that are grown in ways that preserve the soil.

Current Status: A tiny fraction of the original North American grasslands still exist as small, isolated patches scattered through-out the West.

CHAPTER 1

Fire, Drought, and *Tanka*

▼

How can you see something that existed hundreds of years before you were born? How can you understand something that is no longer here? How can you visit a place that may exist in the future?

In your imagination you can see pictures and hear the voices of people who lived before us and those who will come after us. In your mind, with a little help, you can become a time traveler. You can cross America and see what was here before your time and what might be here after you are gone.

Red Knights of the Prairie

The American **prairie** has been home to people for thousands of years. Native Americans, known as the Plains Indians, lived on the **grasslands** for ten thousand years, hunting game and gathering plants for food.

Before European settlers came to the Great Plains of North America, prairies covered most of the American West.

A well-known artist, C. M. Russell, painted this view of a Native American buffalo hunt.

During the 1700s the Plains Indians acquired horses brought to America by Spanish explorers. For two hundred years, the people of the Great Sioux Nation, as they were called, lived on this great sea of grass called the Great Plains.

There were seven Sioux tribes spread over this vast area of North America. But it was the hunters of the Lakota tribe who became known as the Red Knights of the Prairie. They were skilled horsemen who hunted buffalo from horseback. The prairie—or *tinta*, as the Lakota called it—was their home, and they roamed it for hundreds of miles in search of the buffalo, which provided them with almost everything they needed.

The *Tinta*

During the time of the Great Sioux Nation, most of the American West was covered with prairie, or grasslands. Grasslands stretched from Canada in the north to Mexico in the south and from the Rocky Mountains in the west to the shores of the Mississippi river in the east. Grasslands covered the valleys along the West Coast in what is now the state of California. At one time grasslands covered almost one-half of the earth's land surface.

There are different kinds of grasslands all over the world. In Asia and Europe, grasslands are called *steppes* and look like fields of short, bunchy grass. The *pampas* of South America are covered by thousands of miles of tall grass. In Africa, grasslands called *velds* have existed for more than a million years. And in North America, grasslands are divided into different groups depending on their location and climate.

Before settlers came to America from Europe, grasslands covered all of the Great Plains area (see

Shortgrass prairie in Montana.

map). **Shortgrass prairie** stretched from the Rocky Mountains of Colorado to western Kansas—an area in which not much rain falls. Rainfall is higher in central Kansas, and grasses can grow taller. This is where the **mixed-grass prairie** grew. And even farther east—in

Tallgrass prairie in the Flint Hills of Kansas.

Kansas, Iowa, and Illinois—grasses grew very tall—sometimes over ten feet! This area is called the **tallgrass prairie**, and it gets the most rainfall—at least two times as much rain as the shortgrass prairie.

Other areas of North America besides the Great

Plains were covered with grasslands. There were desert grasslands in the Southwest and mountain grasslands farther north.

The grasslands were different from each other in many ways. But they had things in common, too. Grasslands are places where mostly grasses grow. Other plants called **herbs** also grow in grasslands. There are many different kinds, or **species,** of grasses and herbs. A species is a group of plants or animals that are alike. Members of a species look the same and can breed with each other to produce new plants or animals.

In dry grasslands, there may be fifty species of plants on one acre of land. But in grasslands that get more rain, there may be more than two hundred species. There are few trees in grasslands. Trees are plants that cannot survive the dry climate and wind-swept fires of the grassland.

Grasslands are a kind of **ecosystem**. An ecosystem is a place where certain kinds of plants and animals live together. The plants and animals in an ecosystem depend on each other for life. These living things get everything they need from each other and from their surrounding environment.

Fire is an important part of the grassland ecosystem.

Fire!

Hundreds of years ago, people were a part of the grassland ecosystem, too. Native Americans depended on the plants and animals of the grasslands for food, clothing, and tools. These Indian tribes may have even helped the grasslands by setting fires. Fires are an important part of the grassland ecosystem.

On the tallgrass prairie where the Lakota Indians lived, fire could travel 125 miles in one day! Some fires started from lightning striking the dry grass. Others may have been started by Indian campfires.

Fire is very important to grasslands because it burns the dry and dead grass that has been growing for many years. When the old grass is burned, there is room for young grasses to grow.

Before a fire, the soil is covered by thick layers of grass and other plants. Young plants have a hard time growing because the thick layers of grass block out sunshine. Grasses, herbs, and all green plants need sunshine to grow. These plants are able to turn the energy from the sun into food energy used for growing. Without enough sunshine, young plants will die in the shade of taller grasses.

During a fire, the dead and older grasses are burned to the ground, and black ashes cover the soil. But the prairie is not destroyed. Underground the grasses are still alive. Thick roots reach far below the surface, where they soak up water. Bunches of hairy **rhizomes**, which look like underground branches, "creep" under the soil. From the leaflike tips of the rhizomes, new plants poke through the ashes. The sun warms the soil, and new plants quickly sprout in the sunshine.

Plants need **nutrients** as well as sunshine to grow.

Prairie fires release nutrients that help young plants grow.

Nutrients are the parts of any food that help living things grow healthy and strong. In some ecosystems, such as forests, nutrients are put back into the soil when trees rot, or **decompose**. Tiny living things called **microbes** "eat," or decompose, dead trees and plants. When a tree rots, it is broken down into smaller parts. Some of these parts are nutrients, and they are used over and over again by young plants.

The leaves on prairie grasses do not fall to the

ground every year like the dead leaves on trees. Instead, they may wave in the wind for years before being blown off or trampled to the ground by animals. It may be many years before a dead leaf falls to the ground and is broken down into nutrients by the microbes that live in the soil.

But if fire passes through the grassland, the dead leaves are burned away quickly. Some of the nutrients are left in the ashes on top of the soil. Now the nutrients can be used again to help young plants grow.

Fire also kills plants that "steal" nutrients, space, and water from the grasses. Since most trees cannot live through fires, fires prevent trees from growing in grasslands. This allows grasses to grow without **competition** from trees.

Drought

Fire is not the only thing that prevents trees from growing in grasslands. On the prairie there is not enough rain for most trees to grow. Grasses and herbs do not need as much water as trees, and there are times during the year when it doesn't rain for weeks or sometimes months.

When there is a **drought**, fires catch easily in the dry grasses and spread quickly. Fire and drought are two things that make the prairie a grassland ecosystem.

The *Tanka*

The Lakota Indians depended on the buffalo—or *tanka*, as they named the animal—for many of their needs. They went on two big hunts every year, one in the summer and one in the fall. The men killed as many *tanka* as they could with their spears and arrows. But there were always thousands and thousands left.

After the hunt, the people feasted on buffalo meat and organs. Buffalo tongue was a favorite food. There was always a lot of meat left over, and this was dried into jerky or made into *pemmican. Pemmican* was a mixture of meat, fat, and berries pounded together to make a high-energy food that was eaten during the winter.

The women were experts at using every part of the buffalo. Skins were made into clothing, tepees, rope, boats, drums, and bags for carrying things. Bones were made into knives, arrowheads, needles, shovels, scrapers, and smoking pipes. Organs were made into

A Lakota woman preparing a buffalo hide, stretched in a frame.

water bags and cooking pots. Buffalo hooves became rattles, and tails were made into fly swatters. No part of the animal was wasted.

Oh, Give Me a Home . . .

Buffalo were the third important part of the prairie grassland ecosystem. Buffalo are big animals that eat grass. Animals that eat grass are called **grazers**. All grasslands depend on grazers to stay healthy.

Buffalo were not the only grazers on the grasslands. Other large mammals such as pronghorn antelope, deer, and elk roamed the prairies, eating grasses. Mammals are animals with fur or hair on their bodies. They give birth to live young and feed the young with mother's milk.

Smaller animals such as rabbits and grasshoppers are also grazers. But the big grazing mammals were the animals that, together with fire and drought, created the prairie.

The ways in which the buffalo and other grazers helped make the prairie are complicated. Like the famous question "Which came first, the chicken or the egg?" it is hard to know how the grasses and the grazers came to depend on each other.

We do know that grazing animals need large amounts of grass in order to survive. The Great Plains were the perfect **habitat**, or natural living area, for buffalo. Habitat includes food, water, and shelter. On the prairie, there was an unlimited supply of food for the buffalo in the form of grass.

. . . Where the Buffalo Roam

But without the buffalo, the prairie might not have been so large and productive. Buffalo ate the stems and

Grazing buffalo once roamed the Great Plains in herds numbering in the millions.

leaves of grass. These heavy animals also trampled down grasses and other plants as they grazed. When they finished grazing in an area, the tall grass that once waved in the wind was gone.

Like fire, grazing buffalo did not destroy the prairie. Instead, they removed the thick layers of grass and left the soil open to the sunshine. This allowed new plants to sprout out of the ground. In this way, the buffalo helped the prairie renew itself with healthy plants.

Buffalo helped the prairie in other ways. These large grazers ate the tops of plants where the seeds are found. When they finished grazing in one area, they roamed to another one to begin again. But inside their stomachs, they brought seeds from other areas. When they left behind their solid waste, or dung, they also left behind seeds. From these, new plants grew.

Herds of millions of buffalo left behind a lot of dung and urine, or liquid waste. But to the prairie, this was not waste but valuable natural **fertilizer**. Fertilizer is made of nutrients that help plants grow. Buffalo waste contains important nutrients that plants need. The buffalo's cycle of eating plants and then returning nutrients to the soil insured that the prairie remained healthy year after year.

CHAPTER 2

The Good Earth

▼

Native grasslands are rich in **species diversity**, meaning that many different species of plants grow in one area.

Native Americans used more than one thousand different grassland plants as food. Wild plants were a very important part of the Indians' diet. They provided important nutrients that were not found in buffalo and other kinds of meat. Plants also helped feed the Indians through the winter months, when they were unable to hunt the buffalo.

Native American women gathered the wild plants. The women knew where to find each kind of plant. Some plants were cooked and eaten right away, but many plants were hung to dry on strings or stored in leather bags for use during the winter.

Lakota women and children dug prairie turnips, or

A rich variety of native plants grew on the native grasslands of North America.

tipsin, out of the ground during the summer. The roots could be stored for months and even years. *Tipsin* was the most important plant food of the Lakotas—so important that it influenced where they chose their hunting grounds.

Hog peanuts—also called *onmnicha*, which means "ground beans"—were another important food. Boiled, and used in stews, the large white beans were delicious and nutritious. Women often took hog peanuts from the underground stores of a vole (another name for a rodent) known as the bean mouse, or *Hintunka*. This vole digs a hole in the ground and buries hog peanuts for later use. Then it covers the hole with sticks, leaves, and dirt.

Indian women never took the beans without leaving some other food, such as corn or buffalo fat, for the vole. They believed it would be wicked and unfair to take from the voles and leave nothing in return.

Living Roots

Most grassland plants are **perennials**. This means they do not die in the fall of the year like many other plants. Instead, the roots of perennials live all winter under the soil. Many grassland plants live as long as twenty years!

These long-living grassland perennials usually do not reproduce with seeds. **Reproduction** is the way in which living things make babies or young plants, and seeds are used by many plants to reproduce. If a seed is planted in the ground, a new plant will grow.

But grassland plants are different. Even though many grassland plants make seeds, they do not depend on the seeds for their reproduction. Sometimes a new plant might grow from a fallen seed or a seed left behind in a pile of buffalo dung.

Rhizomes live under the soil all winter, and in the spring new plants shoot out of the stems through the soil toward the sunshine.

Small soapweed, called *hupestula* by the Lakotas, is a perennial with bell-shaped white flowers that bloom in May. Indians used many parts of this plant for food: the flower stalk, steamed in spring like asparagus, flower petals in salads, and small fruits in summer.

In the spring, the prairie comes alive with many kinds of wildflowers. Heavy rains coax plants out of the ground. And under the ground, roots catch and soak up the water like a living net. The underground roots of

Wildflowers such as this purple bee balm color the prairie in springtime. Native Americans used bee balm leaves to make tea, medicine, and perfume.

so many different perennial plants help keep prairie soils healthy year after year.

Making Soil

Soil is formed over millions of years, but it can be washed away in seconds by rain. Tangled mats of grassland roots hold the soil firmly and do not let it wash away, even during the heaviest rainstorms.

Soil is made over long, long periods of time. Water, heat, cold, and friction, or rubbing together, all combine to break rock into tiny grains that become one part of soil. But soil is not just made of tiny pieces of rock. Another part of the soil is made of **organic** materials—materials that were once living.

The organic part of soil is the dead remains of plants and animals. When a plant or animal dies, it becomes food for millions of tiny living things.

Bacteria are tiny living things that feed on dead plants and animals. Bacteria help recycle nutrients by breaking down larger animals and plants into tiny pieces. For example, the nutrients in the root of a dead grass plant are put back into the soil when bacteria decompose the root. These nutrients can be used again and again by living plants.

Fungi also help decompose dead remains and make the soil healthy. Fungi are plants that cannot make their own food from the energy of the sun. Instead, they must get their food from dead plants and animals. Like bacteria, many fungi are too tiny to see.

Hundreds of other species of small living things live

in the soil, too. They all help keep it healthy by recycling nutrients and by breaking the earth into tiny
pieces so that air can get inside.

Earthworms are important soil animals. They "eat"
dirt and leave behind nutrient-filled waste. They also
turn the earth over and over, like millions of tiny
shovels. This brings air into the ground, which is needed for the other things that live there.

If you were to dig one shovel of dirt from a grassland, you would find millions of tiny animals. Beetles,
termites, millipedes, centipedes, and mites are all soil
arthropods. These small animals all have a hard outer
skeleton and jointed legs. There are more arthropods
on earth than any other group of animals. Eighty-five
percent of all the animals in the world are arthropods.

Many arthropods eat bacteria and fungi. Some eat
dead plant roots and the dead remains of other
arthropods. Some prey on, or hunt and kill, other
arthropods. All of them help to keep the soil healthy
and rich by recycling nutrients.

A Respect for Nature

Native Americans depended on nature for life. They

had a great knowledge of prairie plants, and they understood which ones were best used for foods, medicines, dyes and paints, and other things. They also had a great respect for the prairie, because they knew they could not survive without the plants and animals that lived there.

The Lakota Indians told how they were taught by their parents and grandparents: "Do not needlessly destroy the flowers on the prairies or in the woods. If the flowers are plucked there will be no flower babies [seeds]; and if there be no flower babies then in time there will be no people of the flower nations. And if the flower nations die out in the world, then the earth will be sad. All the flower nations and all the different nations of living things have their own proper place in the world, and the world would be incomplete and imperfect without them." *

The Newcomers

When the pioneers settled the grasslands, they brought with them plows to turn the soil. They quickly discovered that the soil was black and rich. It was filled with nutrients that helped their planted crops grow.

*(From Melvin Gilmore, *Uses of Plants by the Indians of the Missouri River Region*, University of Nebraska Press, 1919, 1977.)

But Native Americans already knew that the life of the prairie was under the ground. They knew that the soil gave life to all the plants, and that the plants gave life to the buffalo.

There is a story about an old Lakota Indian who watched a pioneer plowing the prairie so it could be planted. "Wrong side up," he said. Once the prairie was plowed, it could never again be a native grassland. The great American grasslands were lost forever.

Plowing the prairies for crops has changed rich grassland ecosystems into seas of waving wheat and corn. The prairies have become the "breadbasket of the world."

CHAPTER 3

Breadbasket of the World

▼

Pioneers pushed westward and made their homes on the fertile soil of the native American grasslands. On the prairies of the Great Plains, they planted corn, wheat, and other grains.

In 1848 gold was discovered in California. A year later, the "forty-niners" followed in search of gold and fortune. They crossed the grasslands, killing buffalo along the way. After the gold rush, the forty-niners made their homes in the rich valleys of California. There they plowed the grasslands and planted fruit trees, grapes, and vegetables.

The Last Buffalo

Along with the wagon trains of pioneers came the railroads and the buffalo hunters. The first railroads began crossing the Great Plains in the 1860s. The rail-

Crops have replaced almost all of the grasslands that once covered large areas of North America.

road workers made a sport of killing buffalo. In the 1870s the railroad companies brought trainloads of hunters, who shot the buffalo from their train seats. The dead buffalo were left to rot on the prairie.

Some hunters shot the buffalo on horseback. Then

This 1871 engraving shows hunters shooting buffalo from a train on the Kansas Pacific Railroad.

they skinned the animals and sold their hides for three dollars each. In 1800 there were sixty million buffalo on the grasslands of the Great Plains. By 1900 there were only one thousand animals left. The killing of the buffalo almost caused them to become **extinct**. Extinction means that a plant or animal is gone from the earth forever. Other large animal species that once grazed on American grasslands were also hunted to near extinction.

As the buffalo disappeared, so did the Native Americans. Tribes such as the Lakota, which depended on buffalo and the plants of the grasslands for survival, were forced to fight for their way of life. But they could not win against the guns and large numbers of white settlers and soldiers.

With the buffalo gone, the Indians faced starvation. They were forced to live on reservations. Their way of life was gone forever.

The grasslands disappeared along with the Native Americans, buffalo, elk, pronghorn antelope, and deer. In the grasslands' place came farms—farms that would someday feed an entire nation, as well as people from all over the world.

Food for Thought

Agriculture, the growing of crops for food, has been practiced for about twelve thousand years. Before agriculture, people hunted animals and gathered plants for food. They had to travel, often great distances, in search of good hunting grounds.

When people learned how to raise their own plants, they no longer had to travel in search of food. Towns

Many kinds of machines are used in modern agriculture.

and cities grew. A few people—the farmers—could grow enough food for everyone in the town. This made it possible for other people to do things besides farming. Machines were invented to help farmers with their work. More and more people could live from the food grown by fewer and fewer farmers. As a result, populations and cities grew.

Before agriculture was invented, there were only eight million people on the entire earth. Now there are more than five hundred times that many—or more than five billion people on the planet. In some places there is not enough food to eat, and people starve. But in most places, people have enough food to survive. Since the United States produces more food than any other nation, it has been called the "breadbasket of the world."

Gone with the Wind . . . and Water

The crops that farmers plant on the grasslands are very different from the wild perennial plants that once grew there. **Grains** such as corn, wheat, and rye are called **annuals**. An annual is planted in the spring and dies in the fall. No part of the plant stays alive through the winter. But the wild perennials of the grasslands lived year-round, under the ground.

Farmers plant seeds to grow annuals. In the fall they harvest the tops of the plants, which contain the seeds. The seeds are used as food, and some of them are saved to plant again in the spring. The stalks and the roots of the plants die. Farmers plow the fields and leave the soil bare and unplanted during the fall and winter.

When the farmer plows the soil, there are no plant

Corn is an annual grain grown for food.

roots to keep it in place. Water and wind carry away the soil, and with it go important nutrients. These can never be put back into the soil. After many years of farming, the soil loses more and more nutrients.

At first the settlers didn't have to worry about losing nutrients from the soil. The soil was rich because grass-

Without plant roots to hold soil in place, wind and water carry it away.

lands had grown on it for many thousands of years. There was so much land that farmers could move to better soil every few years.

But as time went on, the soil began to suffer. Every year the soil lost more nutrients. And every year more soil was washed away by rain because there were no roots and rhizomes underground to hold it in place. This is called **soil erosion**.

Annual crops do not have the deep roots and the tangled rhizomes that wild perennials have. As a result some soil in farm fields is washed away even in summer when crops are planted in the soil. Soil that is not held firmly in place by the roots of plants quickly washes away in the rain and is carried away by streams and rivers.

Chemicals and Crops

Farmers soon learned that they had to add something to the soil to keep their crops growing. In the times of the pioneers, they added the dung from their cows and horses, which contained many important nutrients. But as time went on, this was not enough.

Now farmers add millions of pounds of **chemical fertilizers** to the soil every year. Chemical fertilizers contain important nutrients like **nitrogen** and **phosphorus**. Chemical fertilizers are made from **fossil fuels**, such as oil.

Fossil fuels are rich in nutrients because they are made from materials that were once alive. Fossil fuels are made of the dead remains of partially decayed ancient plants. After millions and millions of years of being buried deep in the earth, the chemicals that were once living plant materials have changed form to become oil, coal, and natural gas.

Insecticides are sprayed on crops to kill plant-eating insects.

Farmers also put other chemicals on crops to keep them growing. **Insecticides** are chemicals that kill insects that eat crops. When it rains, fertilizers and insecticides get washed into streams, rivers, and lakes. This pollutes the water and makes it unsafe to drink in some places.

Farmers have been using chemicals to help them grow crops for about fifty years. Because of chemicals there has been enough food to feed most of the

world's growing population. But now some scientists,
farmers, and other people are starting to wonder how
long we can continue with modern farming methods
before we run out of fossil fuels and pollute much of
our water. Worst of all, they wonder how long the soil
can last before it all washes away.

The ancient grasslands have given us the priceless
gift of fertile soil. We have used that rich soil to feed
the world. But if we lose the soil to erosion, we can
never replace it. That raises a difficult question: How
can we continue to feed the world and save our
precious soil at the same time? Perhaps the answer lies
hidden within native grasslands.

CHAPTER 4

Grassland Islands

▼

Almost all of the grasslands that covered much of North America are gone. In their place are farms, towns, and cities. The pieces of native grasslands that still exist are called islands because they are just small patches.

Some of these island grasslands are strictly protected and cannot be visited. Others are places where people can go to discover what grasslands were like more than one hundred years ago. And a few are places where scientists carry out important research.

The Tallgrass Prairie Preserve

In the Osage Hills of Oklahoma, there is an island of soil that has never been plowed. For more than one hundred years, the land has been grazed by **domestic** animals such as cattle. This land is not a true tallgrass

From a satellite orbiting far above the earth, the Tallgrass Prairie Preserve looks like an empty brown space.

prairie because buffalo and other wild grazers haven't roamed there for more than a century. Fire has not burned the grasses, either.

There is no place left in North America that can be called a true tallgrass prairie. Almost all of the prairie has been plowed for crops. What is left are small pieces that aren't big enough to be a real prairie ecosystem.

The plants we use for food were once wild plants. Over thousands of years, people grew them, and they became domestic crops. But the crops we grow for food are not as strong as wild plants. Domestic plants are more prone to certain diseases and damage by plant-eating insects.

Sometimes scientists discover a wild plant that is very similar to a domestic plant. But the wild plant is stronger than the domestic plant and can fight off diseases and insect pests. Scientists breed, or mate, the wild plant with the domestic plant to get a new kind of plant. The new plant can be grown as food and is also stronger than the domestic parent plant.

This is one reason why it is important to save as many wild plants as we can. We do not know how many wild plants exist that may someday become important food for people.

Many plants are also used as medicine. Scientists are discovering new types of medicines that come from the leaves, roots, and stems of wild plants. If we destroy all the places where wild plants grow, we may be destroying medicines that could save many human lives.

Islands of tallgrass prairie left today are rich in biodiversity.

When an entire ecosystem is preserved, scientists have a chance to see how nature really works. In nature, soil erosion is not a problem. Grasslands do not lose soil to wind and water, because the land is not plowed. Many different kinds of plants are able to grow in grasslands—enough to feed the huge numbers of buffalo and Native Americans that once lived there.

Some scientists think that farmers should try to copy nature and grow crops in the same way that plants grow on the prairie. If they did they would grow many different kinds of plants in one field. The plants would be perennials instead of annuals, and the land would not be plowed. This is a new idea for agriculture. By studying the way the prairie works, scientists may discover a way to grow healthy crops for food without using chemical fertilizers and without losing soil to erosion.

The Carrizo Plain

The Carrizo Plain is only 150 miles away from the city of Los Angeles. It is 180,000 acres of land that has not been plowed for agriculture. There are no big towns nearby, no electric wires, and no telephones. It is a place that has escaped the **development**, or changing of the land by people, that has happened in most of California.

The Carrizo Plain has not been developed because it is nestled between two mountain ranges. The land there has not been plowed and planted with crops because it is very dry and there is no system for bringing in water. It is also a place that gets cold in winter—temperatures sometimes drop below zero.

But the Carrizo Plain is not a wasteland. It is the last island of grassland that once covered more than one-fourth of California. The Carrizo Plain provides a habitat for more **endangered species** than any other place in California. An endangered species is a plant or animal that is in danger of becoming extinct. Most species are endangered because their habitat is disappearing—people are developing the land to use for growing food, grazing animals, and building houses, factories, and stores.

Before the coming of white settlers, native grasses covered the fertile valleys of California. Large animals such as tule elk and pronghorn antelope grazed on the grasslands.

Tule elk once grazed on the grasslands that covered California's fertile valleys.

Now almost all of California's grasslands are gone. In their place are huge farms, towns, and cities. But the Carrizo Plain has been left almost untouched. For the past hundred years, ranchers have grazed cattle there. The cattle have eaten and trampled most of the perennial bunch grass that once covered the plain. In its place, annual grasses grow. But if the plain is protected from heavy grazing, the native grasses might return.

The grasses may grow here again because the Carrizo Plain is being made into a huge **nature preserve**. It will be a place where people can visit. But they will not be allowed to drive cars or all-terrain vehicles. It will be a place where people will be able to see what the native grasslands looked like hundreds of years ago.

It took a lot of cooperation among many people to make sure the Carrizo Plain was protected. The Nature Conservancy was the leader in the plan to protect the plain. It bought almost half of the plain and plans to buy more land. The Bureau of Land Management, which is part of the United States government, owns some of the land and will make sure it is protected. Other pieces of land are owned by people and companies. All of them have agreed to protect the land, too.

The Carrizo Plain will be one of the biggest nature preserves in the United States. It will be a place where people will be able to see and touch a native grassland ecosystem.

CHAPTER 5

A Circle of Life

▼

In nature, living things are **interdependent**. This means they depend on each other for survival. They may depend on each other for food, for shelter, or even for reproduction. On the Carrizo Plain, the San Joaquin kit fox, the giant kangaroo rat, and the blunt-nosed leopard lizard are interdependent. Kit foxes eat giant kangaroo rats. Blunt-nosed leopard lizards use the burrows of giant kangaroo rats to hide from **predators**, which are animals that hunt and kill for food. All three of these species are endangered. If their habitat is not protected, they could become extinct.

Welcome Home!

Pronghorn antelope were once hunted until no animals were left on the Carrizo Plain. But pronghorns live on the Carrizo Plain again! They have been **reintroduced**

Pronghorn antelope have been reintroduced to the Carrizo Plain.

by wildlife biologists (scientists who study animals in their natural habitat). When a wild species is reintroduced, it is taken from one place and brought to another. The species is protected so that it can reproduce like it did before it was hunted by humans.

Some pronghorn antelope were captured in their home range in the northwest corner of California. Then they were driven by truck 650 miles south to their new home on the Carrizo Plain. Biologists hope they will reproduce and run in big herds as they did hundreds of years ago.

Pronghorn antelope are the fastest mammals in the Western Hemisphere. They can run sixty miles per hour! They stand only about three feet tall—about the height of a four-year-old child. They have black horns and a white spot on their rear ends. Pronghorns have excellent eyesight. If you look at them with binoculars, they can see you as well as you can see them!

Some Prairie Birds

Burrowing owls live on the Carrizo Plain. These owls are raptors. Raptors are birds that have strong, notched beaks and sharp claws called talons. Since they hunt small mammals for food, they are predators. The burrowing owl has very long legs for an owl. It makes its nest in empty holes and the burrows of rodents such as giant kangaroo rats.

Other raptors that live on the Carrizo Plain include peregrine falcons, bald eagles (both endangered species), prairie falcons, and hawks.

Raptors live on the prairies of the Great Plains, too. A young bald eagle perches on a tree that grows near a stream on the tallgrass prairie. Its keen eyes can see small mammals in the grass below.

The burrowing owl is one raptor that lives on the Carrizo Plain.

Prairie chickens are the birds most people think of when they think of the tallgrass prairie. Prairie chickens live on the ground and eat seeds. Every year they go to a special place on the prairie to mate. The mating place is large enough for the birds to display their courtship behavior. Courtship behavior is the way in which male birds act to try to attract a female with which to mate.

A male prairie chicken has a bright orange piece of skin on his throat, which he fills with air during court-

The male prairie chicken makes a booming sound with its throat during courtship.

ship. He makes a hollow booming sound, like the sound made when you blow across a soda bottle. The males strut around and fight with each other, too. All this is done to try to impress the females, which strut among the males, looking at them closely.

Only one or two males are chosen as "good enough" by the females. The chosen males mate with all the females. This behavior helps insure that young birds will inherit the "best" **genes**. Genes are passed from parents to their babies, or young. They determine how a living thing will look, how it will behave, and even how healthy it will be.

After mating, a female quickly flies off to build her nest on the ground. Soon she lays a dozen or more eggs, which hatch in less than a month. Young prairie chickens learn to fly when they are two weeks old!

Sometimes prairie chickens get so involved in the courtship that they do not notice predators nearby. Surprise attacks by coyotes, raptors, foxes, and bobcats happen every year.

Bobcats, Buffalo, and "Bambi"

A female bobcat looks like she could be watching some courting prairie chickens. She lives on the prairie and hunts birds and small mammals. Like other bobcats, she usually sleeps for most of the day. Bobcats are nocturnal, which means they are awake mostly at night.

Buffalo or bison are the largest animals on the prairie. Buffalo roam freely in places where they are

protected, such as the Tallgrass Prairie Preserve in Oklahoma. They are huge mammals, weighing up to two thousand pounds. Buffalo eat mostly grass. They can live to be thirty years old, but most live about fifteen to twenty years. In the spring each female gives birth to one yellowish red calf. The calves learn to follow their mothers soon after they are born.

White-tailed deer are also grazing animals. A baby deer, called a fawn, has white spots on its coat to help it blend in with its surroundings.

Some Prairie Plants

People tend to notice large animals, such as birds and mammals. But plants are the living things that make grasslands places of great biological diversity.

Big bluestem is the most common grass on the tallgrass prairie. It can grow to be over ten feet tall. Big bluestem is a favorite grass of grazing animals.

Even though grasslands are covered with blankets of grasses, most of the plant species on grasslands are not grass. Herbs make up most of the plants that live on the prairie. Many herbs are used as medicines and seasonings for food.

A bobcat watches its **prey.**

A bee lights on a fragrant purple bee balm flower.

Purple bee balm flowers bloom all summer. Native Americans used bee balm leaves to make tea, medicine, and perfume, and to flavor food.

At least half of each plant that lives on the grassland is under the ground. Prairie coneflowers have strong, branched roots that extend more than five feet under the soil. This may seem deep, but prairie coneflowers have some of the shallowest roots of prairie plants.

Gifts of the Grasslands

Native grasslands are just one kind of ecosystem on earth. But they have given us great gifts—gifts such as fertile soil. They have given us plants to use as food and medicine. Now it is up to us to preserve the grassland islands that remain. From them we may learn many things about farming and growing food that could help feed the world.

But perhaps the greatest value in preserving the grasslands lies in our need to respect and cherish nature. By doing so, we make a connection with our ancient past, when our ancestors once roamed the grasslands in search of food. By saving the last native grasslands, we are saving part of our natural heritage of life on planet earth.

▼

Chapter 1: Fire, Drought, and *Tanka*

1. <u>Make a United States map showing where native grasslands were before the arrival of European settlers.</u> Use different colors to show where each kind of grassland grew: tallgrass prairie, green; mixed-grass prairie, orange; shortgrass prairie, blue; dry or desert grasslands, brown; mountain grasslands, red.

2. <u>Learn more about the Indians who lived in the American West.</u> Choose an Indian tribe that you would like to learn more about. Here is a list of some tribes (and the area of the country they lived in) to choose from: Sioux (Lakota and Dakota): South Dakota ▾ Arapaho: Wyoming, Colorado, Kansas ▾ Kiowa: Kansas ▾ Pawnee: Kansas, Nebraska ▾ Apache: Oklahoma ▾ Comanche: Texas ▾ Osage: Oklahoma, Missouri ▾ Crow: Montana ▾ Cheyenne: Wyoming, South Dakota ▾ Navaho: Arizona, New Mexico ▾ Mescalero: New Mexico, Texas ▾ Pueblo: New Mexico ▾ Zuni: New Mexico ▾ Hopi: Arizona ▾ Pima: Arizona ▾ Paiute: Nevada, California, Utah ▾ Gosiute: Nevada, Utah

Go to the library and find books about the tribe you have chosen. Draw a map showing where the tribe lived. Write a short report telling what the Indians ate, hunted, what they lived in, and other interesting facts about their culture, or way of life.

Chapter 2: The Good Earth

3. <u>Discover how soil is made by nature.</u>

a. Find two pieces of sandstone or limestone (you can also use pieces of building bricks or concrete). Rub them together over a piece of newspaper. How long does it take to get a teaspoon of tiny rocks?

In nature, soil is made when rocks are rubbed together. Fifteen thousand years ago, great ice sheets (known as glaciers) covered the northern part of the United States. The glaciers rubbed against the rocks and broke off rock particles of all sizes.

b. Heat some water to boiling in the bottom pan of a double boiler. In the top pan, place a small piece of limestone. Heat the rock for at least ten minutes. When the rock is very hot, remove it carefully (using a large spoon) and drop it into a pan of ice water. What happened to the rock?

Changes in temperature help to turn rocks into soil. When a rock is heated by the sun, it expands, or gets bigger. When the rock is cooled, it contracts, or gets smaller. When this happens over and over, the rock cracks and small pieces are broken off.

c. Fill a small glass jar to the top with water. Screw the top on tightly and put the jar in a plastic freezer bag. Put the bag with the jar in it in the freezer (or outside if the temperature is below freezing). Let the water in the jar freeze solid. What happens to the jar?

When water freezes it expands, or gets bigger. Ice pushes outward on the container it is in. If it is in glass, the glass will break. If water is in the crack of a rock and then freezes, the rock will crack to make room for the expanding ice. In this way, cold temperatures help to break rock into smaller pieces.

Chapter 3: Breadbasket of the World

4. <u>The grass that grows on your lawn or in the park is a perennial plant.</u> It grows year after year without having to be re-planted. You can easily see how perennial plants hold soil in place by trying to pull a handful of grass out by its roots. Usually you will get a handful of broken grass. The roots stay firmly planted in the ground.

With a small spade, dig deep into the grass and remove a

piece of sod. Measure how deep the roots extend into the ground. Notice the thick tangles of smaller roots and rhizomes that wind through the soil like a net. Now (with permission of an adult) pull an annual plant up by the roots. Remember that an annual plant must be planted from new seed every year. Vegetables such as beans are annual plants. Compare the roots from the annual plant with the perennial grass.

5. See how plants help prevent erosion.

a. Save two half-gallon-size milk cartons. Wash them out and place them on a table with the spouts open and pointing down. Use a pair of scissors to cut off what is now the top panel. You will now have two rectangular-shaped trays with a spout in one end.

b. Cut a piece of grass (roots and all) to fit into one of the cartons. Put plain soil from the same area in the other carton.

c. Put both cartons on a table so that the spouts hang over the edge. Put a chair under the spouts. On the chair place two empty, wide-mouthed glass jars (in a place where they can catch anything dripping out of the spouts). Prop the cartons up a little by putting a small book or block under each end.

d. Make two sprinkling cans by poking holes in the bottom of plastic milk containers. Fill each container with water. Sprinkle the soil in each box with water at the same time. Watch what happens.

The water that flows into the jar off of the bare soil is muddy. A lot of soil has washed away into the jar. But the water in the jar under the box planted with grass is almost clear. The grass has held the soil in place. Grasses hold soil in place. Other kinds of plants do not do as well as grass. Planted crops like corn, tomatoes, and potatoes leave a lot of the soil exposed. And the exposed soil is easily washed away in the rain.

6. Plant an organic garden. This project will take a lot of

time and work, but in the end you will have delicious vegetables to eat. An organic garden does not use chemicals to help it grow. Instead, natural fertilizers like manure and compost materials are used to enrich the soil. Insecticides are not sprayed on the garden to kill insect pests. To learn more about organic gardening, go to your library and ask the librarian to help you find books that can help you. You will also need adults to help you with this project. It will be a learning experience for them, too!

Chapter 4: Grassland Islands

7. Learn more about conservation. Find out where the nearest office of the Nature Conservancy is located. Call or write to them and ask for information about the land they are trying to preserve near your home. Find out why the land is important for plants and animals. Ask if there are any places near your home that you may visit in order to learn more about nature in your area.

8. Find out what species in your state are listed as endangered. Write a letter to your state department of wildlife, natural resources, or environmental conservation. You can find the address and phone number in the section of the phone book for state government. Ask them to send you a list and information about the endangered species in your state. Find out what is being done to protect the species' habitats.

9. Visit a nature preserve near your home. While you are there, try to use all your senses to experience nature. Take deep breaths of fresh air. What smells are in the air? Can you smell blooming flowers or the scent of pine trees? Feel the soil with your hands. Try to imagine what it was like to be alive a long time ago, when people were more connected with their environment. When you get home, write a poem or short story about your visit.

Chapter 5: A Circle of Life

10. <u>Make a poster showing some of the species that live on grasslands.</u> Use crayons, paints, or colored markers to make your poster colorful and bright. When it is finished, hang your poster where it can be seen by others.

11. <u>Make a card game.</u> Have you ever played Go Fish? You can make your own game by drawing pictures on index cards of the species listed in the chapter. Make sure to draw two cards that are exactly the same for each species. When finished, shuffle the cards. Deal the cards out so that each person gets four cards. Put the rest of the cards in a pile on the table. Try to make matches by asking the other players for a card. Go Fish in the pile if they don't have the card. The person who makes the most matches and runs out of cards first wins.

Environmental Organizations

If you would like to learn more about the grasslands discussed in this book or grasslands in general, write to the organizations listed below:

California Field Office
The Nature Conservancy
785 Market Street
San Francisco, CA 94103

Grassland Heritage Foundation
5450 Buena Vista
Shawnee Mission, KS 66205

The Land Institute
2440 East Water Well Road
Salina, KS 67401

Oklahoma Field Office
The Nature Conservancy
320 South Boston, Suite 846
Tulsa, OK 74103

Glossary

agriculture—growing of crops for food.

annual—a plant that grows from a new seed every year.

arthropods—a very large group of small animals with hard, outer skeletons and jointed legs. Eighty-five percent of the earth's animals are arthropods.

bacteria—tiny living things that live in the soil and inside and on other plants and animals. Bacteria help decompose dead materials; they can also cause diseases in living things.

biological diversity—many different living things living in one area; also known as biodiversity or species diversity.

chemical fertilizer—a nutrient-rich material put in the soil to help crops grow. Chemical fertilizers are made from fossil fuels that are rich in the nutrients nitrogen and phosphorus.

competition—used here to mean the way living things struggle or fight for food, water, and places to live.

conservation—saving something for the future; energy conservation means saving energy, such as oil, so there will be enough for use in the future.

decompose—to rot or break down dead plants or animals.

development—the act of people changing the land from its natural state into places that are used for growing crops, grazing animals, and building houses, stores, and factories.

domestic—used here to mean animals that have been "tamed" or plants that have been changed so they can be raised by humans.

drought—a long period during which there is no rain or snow.

ecosystem—a place where animals and plants live and depend on each other for survival. Examples of ecosystems are grasslands, forests, the tundra, and a coral reef.

endangered species—a species, or group, of living things that is in danger of becoming extinct.

extinct—no longer living anywhere on earth.

fertilizer—a nutrient-rich material that is put in the soil to help plants grow. Organic fertilizer is not made from chemicals but instead is made from things that were once living or that come from living things.

fossil fuels—materials such as oil, coal, and natural gas that can be burned to release energy. They are also made into chemical fertilizers because they are rich in important nutrients. They are really the fossils, or dead remains of plants, that lived millions of years ago.

fungi—plants that cannot make their own food from the energy of the sun. Fungi feed on the dead remains of other plants and animals. Many are very small and live in the soil.

genes—the parts of every living thing that are passed from the parents to their young. Genes decide how a living thing will look, behave, and almost everything else about it.

grains—grasses that have been domesticated by people and used for food. Wheat, corn, and rye are grains.

grassland—a kind of ecosystem in which grasses are the most common plants, where trees cannot grow, and where there is a limited supply of water.

grazers—animals that eat grass for food.

habitat—the area in which a plant or animal naturally lives. Habitat provides living things with everything they need for survival—food, water, shelter, and protection.

herb—plant whose stem withers away to the ground after each season's growth; different from a tree or shrub, whose stems live year to year.

insecticides—chemicals that kill insect pests. They are sprayed on crops to prevent insects from eating them.

interdependent—depending upon or needing other animals or plants for survival.

microbes—tiny living things, such as bacteria and fungi, that help decompose dead organic matter.

mixed-grass prairie—the area between the tallgrass prairie and the shortgrass prairie, where there is enough rainfall to support taller grasses; mostly in central Kansas and Nebraska.

nature preserve—a place where habitat is protected from development. Plants and animals are allowed to live in their natural surroundings without people.

nitrogen—a nutrient needed for growth by all plants.

nutrients—parts of food that living things need for growth.

organic—something that was once alive or came from a living thing.

perennial—a plant that lives for more than one year. Its roots stay alive under the soil even if the leaves die.

phosphorus—a nutrient needed for growth by all plants.

prairie—another name for grassland.

predator—an animal that hunts and kills other animals for food.

prey—an animal that is hunted and killed for food.

reintroduced species—animals that are taken from one place and moved to another place. Usually they were all killed in one area by people or their habitat was destroyed, and they are being brought back to a place where they once lived.

reproduction—to make more of the same species.

rhizomes—the underground stems of perennial plants that can "sprout" through the soil and make new plants.

shortgrass prairie—the prairie where grasses could not grow very tall because of the dry climate; the area stretched from the Rocky Mountains of Colorado to western Kansas.

soil erosion—the loss of soil from the earth. Most erosion takes place when bare soil is washed away by rain.

species—a group of living things that are alike. They can breed with each other to reproduce.

species diversity—many different kinds of living things living in one area; also known as biological diversity or biodiversity.

tallgrass prairie—eastern part of the Great Plains, including Kansas, Iowa, and Illinois, where the tallest grasses grew.

Index

▼